ALL ABOUT DINOSAURS

PTERODACTYL

BookLife

by
Amy Allatson

©2017
Book Life
King's Lynn
Norfolk PE30 4LS

ISBN: 978-1-78637-061-7

Written by:
Amy Allatson

Edited by:
Charlie Ogden

Designed by:
Natalie Carr

CONTENTS

Words that appear like this can be found in the glossary on page 23.

PAGE 4	What Were Dinosaurs?
PAGE 6	When Were Dinosaurs Alive?
PAGE 8	Pterodactyl
PAGE 10	What Did the Pterodactyl Look Like?
PAGE 12	Where Did the Pterodactyl Live?
PAGE 14	What Did the Pterodactyl Eat?
PAGE 16	The Biggest and the Smallest Pterosaur
PAGE 18	How Do We Know…?
PAGE 20	Facts About the Pterodactyl
PAGE 22	Draw Your Own Dinosaur
PAGE 23	Glossary
PAGE 24	Index

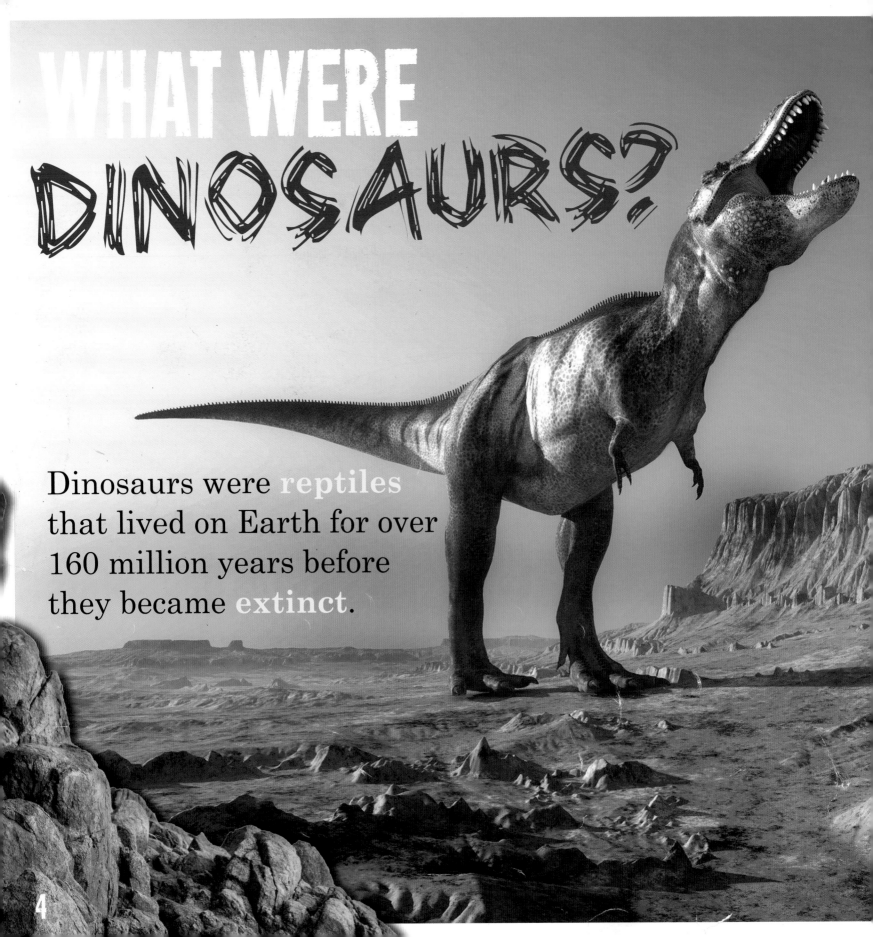

WHAT WERE DINOSAURS?

Dinosaurs were reptiles that lived on Earth for over 160 million years before they became extinct.

There were many different types of dinosaur.
They lived both on land and in water –
and some could even fly!

5

WHEN WERE DINOSAURS ALIVE?

Dinosaurs first lived around 230 million years ago during a period of time called the **Mesozoic** period. The last dinosaurs became extinct around 65 million years before humans were alive.

All land on Earth was together in one piece during the time of the dinosaurs. Over time it has slowly split up into different **continents**.

WHEN ALL THE LAND ON EARTH WAS TOGETHER IN ONE PIECE IT WAS CALLED PANGEA.

EURASIA

NORTH AMERICA

PACIFIC

SOUTH AMERICA

AFRICA

PACIFIC

INDIA

ANTARTICA

PANGEA

PTERODACTYL

NAME	Pterodactyl (te-ro-dack-til)
WINGSPAN	Up to 1 metre
WEIGHT	Up to 5 kilograms
FOOD	Carnivore
WHEN IT LIVED	65–150 million years ago
HOW IT MOVED	Flew and walked on land

Pterodactyls were part of a family of flying dinosaurs called Pterosaurs (te-ro-saws), which first appeared around 150 million years ago. Pterodactyls became extinct around 65 million years ago.

There were lots of different types of Pterosaur. The Pterodactyl was quite small, but other Pterosaurs could grow very large.

PTERODACTYL

THE NAME PTERODACTYL MEANS 'WINGED FINGER'.

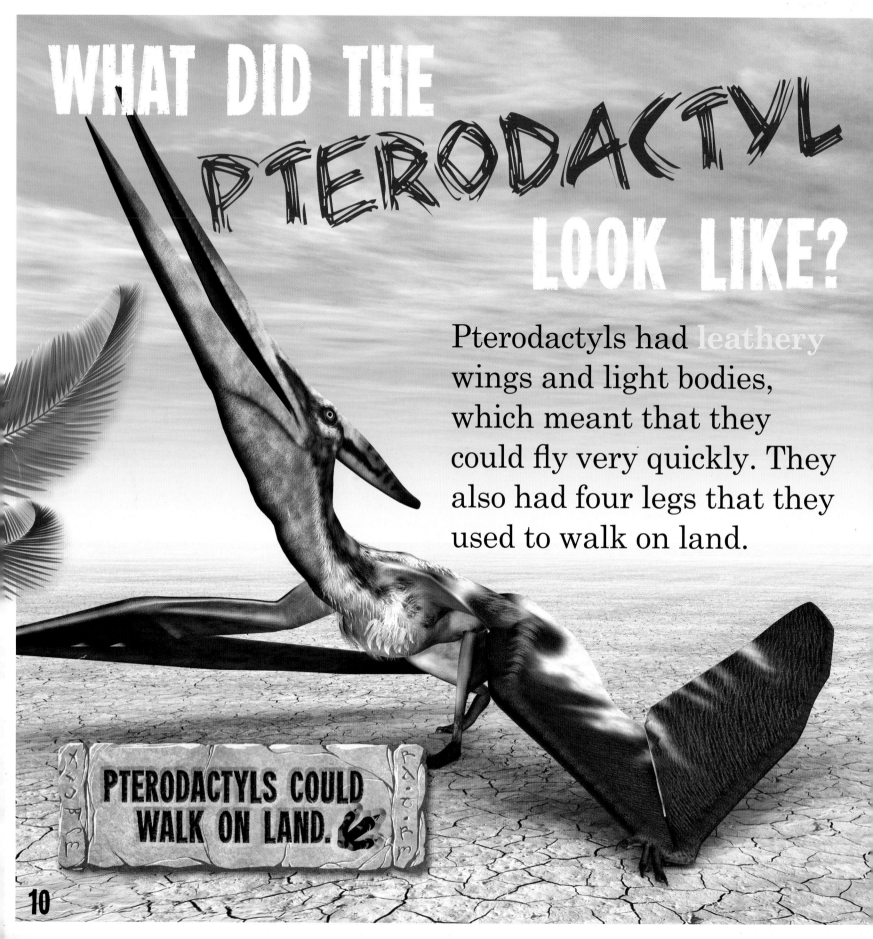

WHAT DID THE PTERODACTYL LOOK LIKE?

Pterodactyls had leathery wings and light bodies, which meant that they could fly very quickly. They also had four legs that they used to walk on land.

PTERODACTYLS COULD WALK ON LAND.

CREST

LONG BEAK

Pterodactyls had long beaks for scooping up fish from the water and a long, pointed crest on the back of their heads.

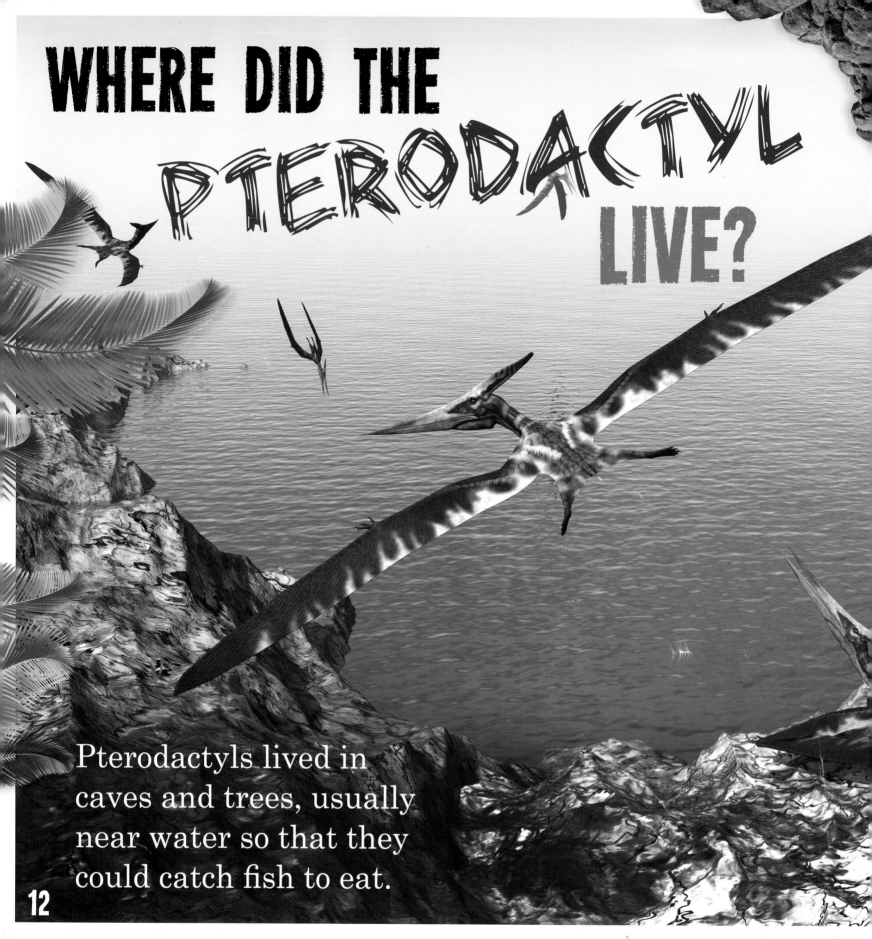

WHERE DID THE PTERODACTYL LIVE?

Pterodactyls lived in caves and trees, usually near water so that they could catch fish to eat.

Pterodactyls lived in many parts of the world. Their fossils have been found in parts of Europe and Africa.

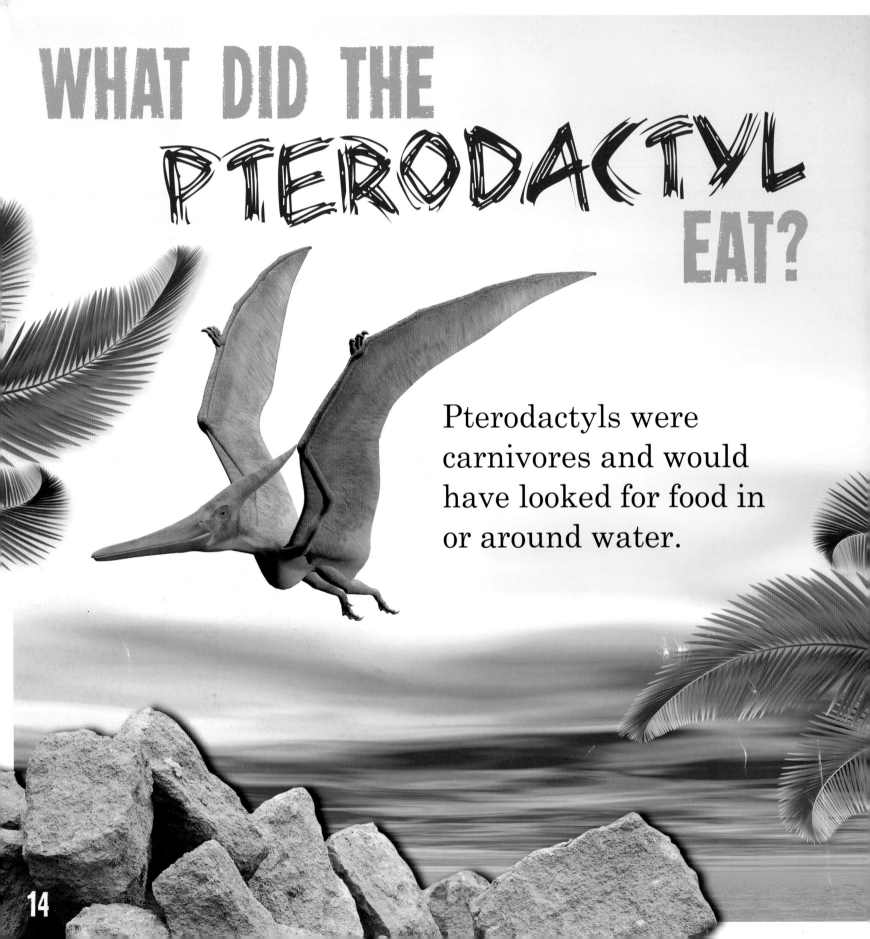

WHAT DID THE PTERODACTYL EAT?

Pterodactyls were carnivores and would have looked for food in or around water.

They ate fish, insects and other small animals such as lizards.

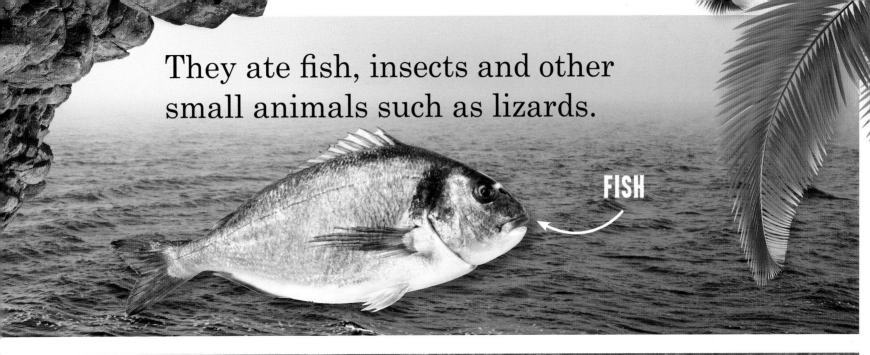

FISH

INSECT

LIZARD

THE BIGGEST AND THE SMALLEST

PTEROSAUR

Some dinosaurs in the Pterosaur family were very big. The Pteranodon (te-ran-o-don) could have a wingspan of up to 7 metres.

THE PTERANODON'S WINGSPAN WAS THE SAME AS THE HEIGHT OF A FULLY GROWN GIRAFFE!

PTERANODON

However, the Nemicolopterus (nem-ee-col-op-tare-us) was much smaller than Pteranodon. It had a wingspan of only 25 centimetres.

PTERANODON

NEMICOLOPTERUS

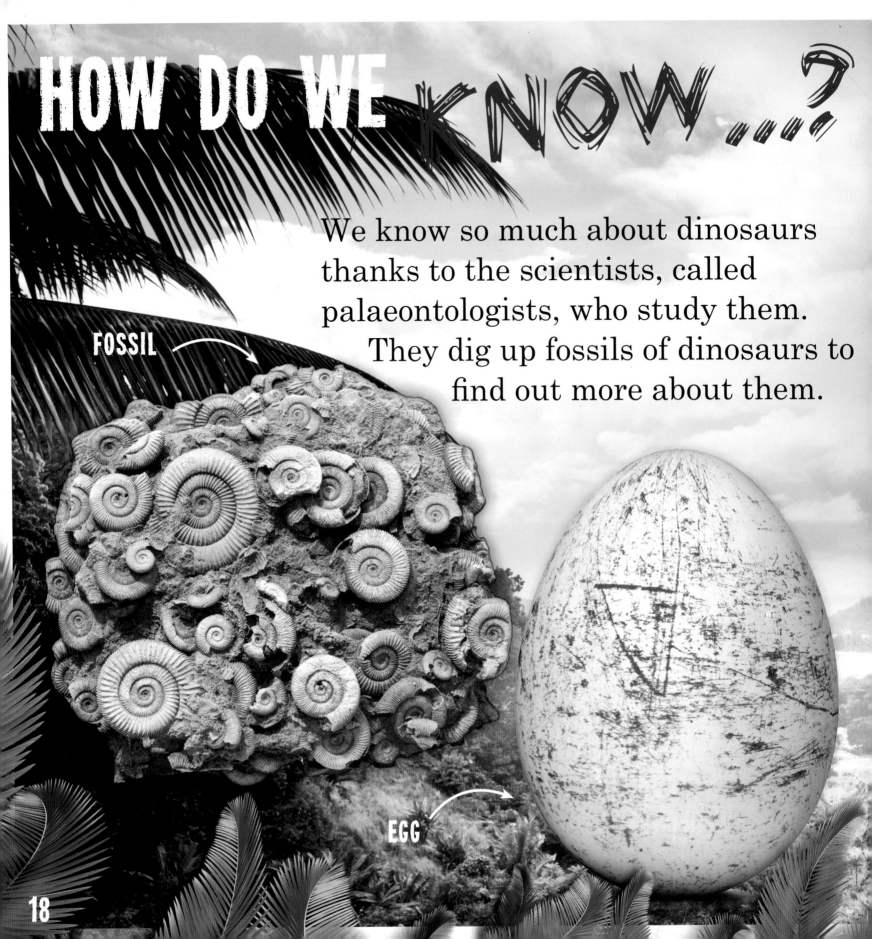

HOW DO WE KNOW...?

We know so much about dinosaurs thanks to the scientists, called palaeontologists, who study them. They dig up fossils of dinosaurs to find out more about them.

FOSSIL

EGG

Scientists put together the bones they find to try and make the full skeletons of dinosaurs. From these skeletons scientists can often work out the size and weight of a dinosaur. We can also find out information about what it ate from its fossilised food and poo.

SKELETON

SCIENTISTS EVEN FIND FOSSILISED EGGS AND FOOTPRINTS BELONGING TO DINOSAURS.

FACTS ABOUT THE PTERODACTYL

LEATHERY WINGS

SOME PTERODACTYLS' BEAKS HAD SHARP TEETH.

LONG BEAK

PTERODACTYLS HAD TAILS, BUT THEY WERE VERY SHORT.

UP TO A 1 METRE WINGSPAN

DRAW YOUR OWN DINOSAUR

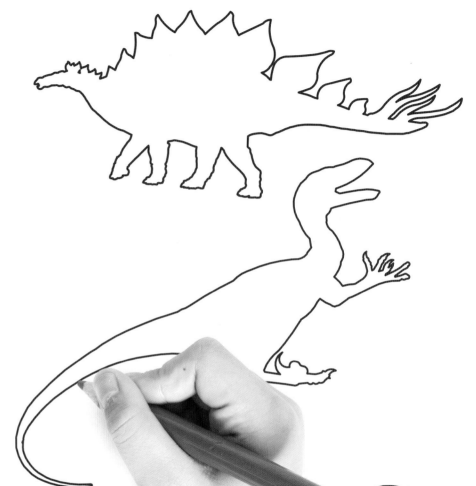

THINK ABOUT THESE QUESTIONS ...

1. How does it move?

2. Does it live on land or in water?

3. What does it eat?

4. What colour is it?

5. How big is it?

GLOSSARY

carnivore an animal that feeds on other animals

continents very large areas of land that are made up of many countries, like Africa and Europe

extinct an animal that is no longer alive

fossils the remains of plants and animals that lived a long time ago

leathery a tough, hard texture that feels and looks like leather

Mesozoic a period of time when dinosaurs lived

reptile a cold-blooded animal with scales

INDEX

Africa 13

beaks 11, 21

carnivores 8, 14

Earth 4, 7

Europe 13

extinct 4, 6, 8

food 8, 14, 19

fossils 13, 18–19

humans 6

land 5, 7–8, 10

palaeontologists 18

reptiles 4

skeletons 19

PHOTO CREDITS

Abbreviations: l-left, r-right, b-bottom, t-top, c-centre, m-middle.

2-3 Suzi44. 4-5 Catmando. 6-7 boscorelli. 8m - Philll. 8-9 background - Alexandra Lande. 9m - Valentyna Chukhlyebova. 10 - Michael Rosskothen. 11 - Elenarts. 12 - Elenarts. 13 - andrea crisante. 14 - Paul B. Moore. 15t background - Scandphoto. 15tm - gajdamak. 15m background - Pure Worx. 15m -jhy. 15b background - Chatrawee Wiratgasem. 15bm - Blinka. 16 - Photobank gallery. 17 background - Alexandra Lande. 17m - Catmando. 18 - 19 background - Iakov Kalinin. 18ml - MarcelClemens. 18br - guysal. 19m - Marques. 20 -21m - Valentyna Chukhlyebova.

Images are courtesy of Shutterstock.com. With thanks to Getty Images, Thinkstock Photo and iStockphoto.